HELICOPTERS
A First Look

PERCY LEED

GRL Consultant, Diane Craig, Certified Literacy Specialist

Lerner Publications ◆ Minneapolis

Educator Toolbox

Reading books is a great way for kids to express what they're interested in. Before reading this title, ask the reader these questions:

What do you think this book is about? Look at the cover for clues.

What do you already know about helicopters?

What do you want to learn about helicopters?

Let's Read Together

Encourage the reader to use the pictures to understand the text.

Point out when the reader successfully sounds out a word.

Praise the reader for recognizing sight words such as *in* and *the*.

TABLE OF CONTENTS

Helicopters 4

You Connect! 21
STEM Snapshot 22
Photo Glossary 23
Learn More 23
Index 24

Helicopters

Helicopters fly high and fast.
They fly low and slow.

They can stay in one spot in the air.

What else can land in small spaces?

They can land in small spaces.

They have long blades.
The blades spin.
This lifts the helicopter.

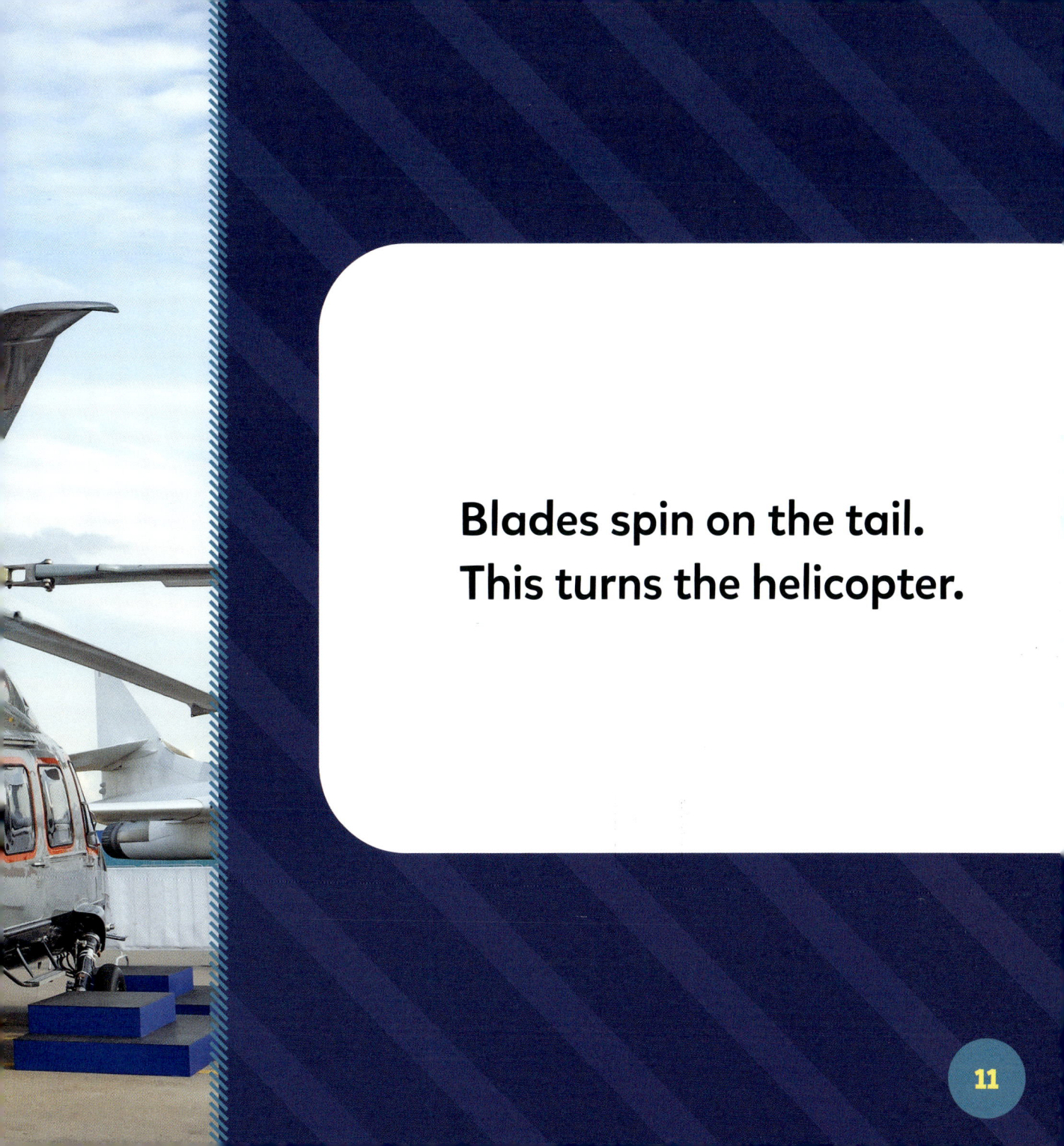

Blades spin on the tail.
This turns the helicopter.

The pilot sits in the cockpit.

The pilot flies the helicopter.

Helicopters help with jobs.
They help people take pictures.

How does flying help people take pictures?

They help people who are hurt or sick. They bring them to a doctor.

When would a hurt person need a helicopter?

They put out fires.

They help find missing people.

Helicopters save lives.

You Connect!

Have you ever been in a helicopter?

Would you want to be a helicopter pilot?

How can you learn more about helicopters?

STEM Snapshot

Encourage students to think and ask questions like scientists. Ask the reader:

What is something you learned about helicopters?

What is something you noticed about helicopter parts?

What is something you still want to learn about helicopters?

Photo Glossary

Learn More

Brody, Walt. *How Military Helicopters Work*. Minneapolis: Lerner Publications, 2020.

Dittmer, Lori. *Helicopters*. Mankato, MN: Creative Education, 2019.

McDonald, Amy. *Helicopters*. Minneapolis: Bellwether Media, 2022.

Index

blades, 9, 11

cockpit, 12

help, 14, 15, 16, 19

land, 7

pilot, 12, 13

tail, 11

Photo Acknowledgments

The images in this book are used with the permission of: © EB Adventure Photography/Shutterstock Images, pp. 4–5; © budgetstockphoto/iStockphoto, p. 6; © pichitstocker/iStockphoto, p. 7; © malexeum/iStockphoto, pp. 8–9; © Dikuch/iStockphoto, pp. 9, 23 (blades); © aapsky/iStockphoto, pp. 10–11, 23 (tail); © Kiselev Andrey Valerevich/Shutterstock Images, pp. 12, 23 (cockpit); © Pasu Ratprasert/Shutterstock Images, pp. 13, 23 (pilot); © yarn/iStockphoto, pp. 14–15; © Monkey Business Images/Shutterstock Images, pp. 16–17; © Toa55/iStockphoto, p. 18; © Christopher Ames/iStockphoto, p. 19; © DanCardiff/iStockphoto, p. 20.

Cover Photograph: © nullplus/iStockphoto

Design Elements: © Mighty Media, Inc.

Copyright © 2024 by Lerner Publishing Group, Inc.

All rights reserved. International copyright secured. No part of this book may be reproduced, stored in a retrieval system, or transmitted in any form or by any means—electronic, mechanical, photocopying, recording, or otherwise—without the prior written permission of Lerner Publishing Group, Inc., except for the inclusion of brief quotations in an acknowledged review.

Lerner Publications Company
An imprint of Lerner Publishing Group, Inc.
241 First Avenue North
Minneapolis, MN 55401 USA

For reading levels and more information, look up this title at www.lernerbooks.com.

Main body text set in Mikado a Medium.

Imperial Public Library
PO BOX 307
Imperial, TX 79743

Library of Congress Cataloging-in-Publication Data

Names: Leed, Percy, 1968–author.
Title: Helicopters : a first look / Percy Leed.
Description: Minneapolis : Lerner Publications , [2024] | Series: Read about vehicles (Read for a better world) | Includes bibliographical references and index. | Audience: Ages 5–8 | Audience: Grades K–1 | Summary: "Helicopters are small and have blades instead of wings. Their size can make them very useful for all sorts of jobs. Full-color photographs and leveled text show readers all the things that helicopters can do"— Provided by publisher.
Identifiers: LCCN 2022035561 (print) | LCCN 2022035562 (ebook) | ISBN 9781728491448 (library binding) | ISBN 9798765603635 (paperback) | ISBN 9781728499864 (ebook)
Subjects: LCSH: Helicopters—Juvenile literature.
Classification: LCC TL716.2 .L44 2023 (print) | LCC TL716.2 (ebook) | DDC 629.133/352—dc23/eng/20220930

LC record available at https://lccn.loc.gov/2022035561
LC ebook record available at https://lccn.loc.gov/2022035562

Manufactured in the United States of America
1 – CG – 7/15/23